Gift before the gift

The holiday season is upon us. This little book is designed to help you walk into the season with perhaps a new sense of what the Lord is saying in and through, not just the holiday; but life.

We know you don't have a lot of time, so each day's reading will take about five minutes. You can leave it at that. Read and be on your way.

Or you can take the thought with you as you go about your business. You might find that the Lord uses it on the road. You might come back to it in the evening and dig a bit deeper using scripture as your guide. Maybe you will talk about it with a friend.

Each day includes a few lines for journaling. If you are reading the ebook version we left the journaling lines in as an encouragement for you to take a few minutes and write out your thoughts, whatever they may be.

There are no rules here. *This book is meant to be a gift before the gifts.* It is *for* you and we are hoping that it is *from* Him in some sense, just because He loves you.

Enjoy

Randy and Amy

About the Authors

Randy Schlichting

Randy has been blessed to participate in kingdom building at Perimeter Church for over 15 years under the leadership of Randy Pope. He has developed and led various ministries including discipleship and worship. Currently he serves as the Pastor of Shepherding.

He has been joyfully married to Dorothy for thirty one years. They love to minister together and they love the beach. Together they have three daughters; two wonderful son in laws and a beautiful grand daughter

Amy Shirley

Amy is a life-long member of Perimeter Church which is where the collaboration for this book began. She is a freelance writer and enjoys working on a variety of writing projects.

She has been married to her college sweetheart, Josh for more than eight years. They enjoy serving together at the church and cheering on their favorite football team.

One - Yes or Better

As you begin this book, we would love for you to commit to pray as you read. To that end, we thought it would be good to start by dealing with some misconceptions about prayer.

A few days before her untimely death, Janis Joplin recorded, a song that went like this: *"O Lord won't you buy me a Mercedes Benz? My friends all drive Porsches I must make amends. Worked hard all my lifetime, no help from my friends, so oh Lord won't you buy me a Mercedes Benz?"* If you have heard it, I am sure Joplin's raspy voice, belting it out a capella, is now back in your head, as you recall the next part of the song, *"Oh Lord won't you buy me a color TV?"* They really are creative prayer lyrics, but not prone to be answered in the affirmative. Joplin knew that. So what type of prayer *would* get a, "Yes!" from the Almighty?

Questions about prayer abound: What should I pray for? Why are my prayers not answered? How come I never have a desire to pray? Some people even ask, "If God knows everything, why should we pray at all?" Good questions.

Have you ever thought that perhaps part of His plan *requires* prayer? Now our prayers are not the initial cause of His actions but they do cause Him to act. Because of His character, He must respond when we pray. In other words, He cannot have a "Nobody Home" sign on His door. So the real question is,

"How will He answer?" Now get this: as odd as it first may sound, He will answer one of two ways to the person who calls on Him in faith: *Yes or Better.* The challenge is seeing that if the answer is not yes, *it is better.*

Think about this: Jesus says He is not going to give us a stone if we ask for bread. He will do right by us. Through His perfect knowledge of what is best for us, He will direct, and decide perfectly. He loves His people and He always does what is best for them, in accordance with His glory.

So, as you start this reader *and* as you enter into this season, we encourage you to pray. Start with some adoration and then maybe a little confession. Next you might want to move along to some thanksgiving. We can all park there for a while. Then you may want to wind up by asking for what you think has value. Be confident that God will say *Yes or Better.*

C.S. Lewis once said that he was glad God had not answered yes to many of his prayers. God had better in mind and, over time, Lewis could look back and see that, in fact, that was indeed the case.

Daniel 9 | Nehemiah 9 | Ezra 9

_____

_____

_____

_____

Two — Give Thanks

Have you ever wondered why some people love Thanksgiving so much? I have talked to many people who say that they enjoy Thanksgiving more than Christmas because it is less focused on what we get and more on what we have been given. In a way, that sounds strange because giving and receiving gifts can be enjoyable. However, without a thankful heart, gifts may eventually reveal their natural essence: they are just things and cannot satisfy. No doubt, God wants us to have a thankful heart. Our problem is that in our fast paced lives we rarely stop and focus our hearts towards the One to whom we should be eternally grateful. So how can we to stop long enough to feast on what is good for our souls? Thanksgiving!

In my family, we all gather in the kitchen before Thanksgiving dinner. We go around and everyone shares something that they are thankful for. It is a special time to celebrate and give thanks for the blessings that each of us has experienced over the past year. Some of the things are simple and some are profound.

Now lest you think that I happen to have the perfect family that always gets what we want, let me assure you that we have had some challenging times. And we have had to learn to be thankful, even for the sad things. That really is difficult to do. Sometimes we can see that struggles brought us something wonderful in return, other times there is no obvious reason or blessing that is accompanying hardship, it's just hard. So this year once again, I join with you as we learn that no matter how trying the past year has been, there is something that we can find to be thankful about: even if it is simply the fact that we have the common graces of air, eyesight, hearing, some health, a roof over our heads, food to eat, and some friends.

I hope that is helpful. It is good and healthy to spend extended time in thanksgiving once a year but we don't need to wait until the leaves turn golden and weather turns cool to have a thankful heart. How would our lives be different if we chose to be truly thankful all through the year and stopped to thank the Lord on a regular basis for His blessings? I think we know we would be happier, more contented people. It doesn't have to be a big sweeping event every day. It could be a short and simple prayer of thankfulness, daily re-focusing our lives on the things above.

A small habit could result in big-time heart change. So what is stopping us? Us. We have a tendency to look on the dark side and it drags us down. That is no way to live. So, can I encourage you to start a new habit? Think of one thing to be thankful for each day. Write it down, share it with a friend, and pray it back to God. That could promote a spirit of gratitude that would be contagious.

Isaiah 12:4 | 2 Corinthians 4:14-16 | Colossians 3:14-16

Three – More Than A Day of Thanksgiving

Bradford, Washington, and Lincoln thought we, as Americans, needed to be spurred on to gratitude and each in turn wrote a proclamation calling for a day of thanksgiving. They were leaders who looked at the landscape and saw that there was much for which to be thankful. In fact, they felt so strongly about it that they made it a national event.

We have just experienced that holiday, institutionalized as Thanksgiving Day. How did we do? For what were we thankful and how did we express it? My guess is most of us prayed a prayer of thanksgiving at the meal where our families and friends gathered together while the turkey, mashed potatoes, gravy, pumpkin pie, and lots of other high-fat food waited to be consumed. A thanksgiving prayer is a good place to start.

After dinner, some of us watched a little football on TV, took an afternoon nap, and maybe even a short walk to "work off the calories." We may have expressed some thanks for the time of rest and enjoyment. That was the right second step.

Now may be time for the third step. Thanksgiving is not over. The Apostle Paul wrote, "Be joyful always, pray continually, give thanks in all circumstances, for this is God's will for you in Christ Jesus" (1 Thessalonians 5:18). Give thanks in all circumstances - that includes weekdays.

The Pilgrims may have recalled Paul's words after their disastrous first year in the new world. They were people who did not have a *day* of thanksgiving; they strived to live *lives* of thanksgiving. They were followers of Christ, who had come to a hard place for freedom, and they nearly died in the process. That is why they were specifically thanking God; for life in Christ. Washington and Lincoln also were thanking God for specific events, but they were not saying that a single day was sufficient and that we should quickly move on to the Christmas shopping season.

All of these men were calling people to a life of thanksgiving in whatever circumstances. Thanksgiving Day is just a starting, or better, a re-starting point to a life of remembering our Creator and blessing Him daily, even hourly, for His common grace and His favor to us as His people. That is the heart of Thanksgiving. We encourage you, as you head back to shopping and life, to think of how you can be thankful because the circumstances could be intriguing for you and your family this season. They may even be hard. How might you do that? Paul gives us a clue, after telling us it is God's will for us to be thankful, when he says, "...in Christ Jesus." It is His birth we will now celebrate as we await His return. In Him and through Him, we can be thankful.

Psalm 147:7 | Colossians 3:16 | Hebrews 12:28

_____
_____
_____
_____

Four - A Humble Prayer by Philip Doddridge modernized by R Schlichting

He was a contemporary of Isaac Watts and George Whitefield; one of those 18th century men that God used to shape the church. He was a theologian, an educator and a man of prayer. We thought it might be helpful for you to pray a prayer written by him. And perhaps you might begin to write some of your prayers as the Lord prompts. Here you go:

"Blessed God! I sincerely acknowledge before you my own weakness and insufficiency to begin anything that is spiritually good. I have failed a thousand times; and yet my foolish heart would again 'trust itself,' (Prov. 28:26) and form resolutions in its own strength. So, I ask that this be the first fruit of your gracious influence upon my heart: to bring it to a humble distrust of itself and to a rest in you! I rejoice, O Lord, in the kind assurances, which you give me of your readiness to bestow liberally and richly so great a benefit to my heart. I do therefore, according to your condescending invitation, come with boldness to your throne, that I may find grace to help in every time of need. (Heb. 4:16)

I mean not, O Lord God, to turn your grace into a license for immorality or perverseness or to make my weakness an excuse for negligence and sloth. I confess that you have already given me more strength than I have used! I charge it upon myself, and not on you, that I have even recently received still more grace from you through your Word and the Spirit. I desire for the future to be found diligent in the use of all appointed means of grace. When I neglect the grace you have given me, petitions like these become a profane mockery, and they might even provoke you to take away what I have, rather than prevail upon you to give me more. But firmly resolving to exert myself to the utmost to use the grace you have given, I earnestly ask for more grace, that I may be enabled to fulfill that resolution.

Be surety, O Lord, to me your servant for good. (Psa. 119:122) Be pleased to shed your sanctifying influences on my soul, to form me for every duty you require. Implant, I ask you, grace and virtue deep in my heart. Bear with me in the midst of me foolishly assaulting your grace. I know I will continue from time to time to do that while I am still in this world and carry about with me so much sin.

Fill me with good affections towards you, my God, and towards my fellow-creatures. Remind me always of your presence, and may I remember that every secret sentiment of my soul is open to you. May I therefore guard against the first risings of sin, and the first approaches to it. May I guard that Satan may not find room for his evil suggestions. I earnestly beg that you Lord, would fill my heart with your Holy Spirit. Dwell in me, and walk with me, and let my body be the temple of the Holy Ghost.

May I be so joined to Jesus my Lord, as to be one with him, (1 Cor. 6:17) and feel His invigorating influences continually bearing me on, superior to every temptation and to every corruption. So that while young people shall faint and grow weary, I may so wait upon the Lord as to renew my strength, (Isaiah 40:30,31) and may go on from one degree of faith, and love, and zeal, and holiness, to another.

_____
_____
_____
_____
_____
_____
_____
_____
_____

Five - Instead of Sheep

"...I count my blessings instead of sheep.
And I fall asleep counting my blessings."
- Count Your Blessings, White Christmas,
Irving Berlin, 1954

It is an Oscar nominated song from one of my favorite Christmas movies of all time, *White Christmas.* In the movie, Rosemary Clooney's character is worried about everything under the sun and as a result she can't sleep. Bing Crosby's character, suggests that instead of thinking about the things that trouble her that she think about all the blessings that she has instead.

In a way, this reminds me of the story of Mary and Martha when Jesus came to visit. Martha was busy thinking about all the things that had to be done and busily worked in the kitchen. Mary recognized the blessing of having Jesus in her home and took the opportunity to sit at his feet and listen to him. She let the world fade away and the only thing that she was focused on was Him. Maybe you are saying, "Hey wait a minute, there are things that need to get done during the holidays. Are you suggesting that we just ignore responsibilities?" Well yes and no. No, I am not suggesting that you completely ignore responsibilities and things that have to get done. But yes, I am suggesting that it may be appropriate from time to time to stop the rushing and rest.

With all of the Christmas cards, holiday parties, and gifts to buy have you found yourself running on empty or feeling that you are missing the blessing of the holiday season? Do you get lost in the busy nature of the Christmas season or really just life in general forgetting that we can and need to come and rest at the feet of Jesus? When was the last time you stopped what you were doing in the midst of stress and worries and sought rest in Him? Are you Mary, Martha, or somewhere in between?

Can I encourage you to try today even just for a few minutes to stop, let the worries of the day fade, and meet with Jesus? Whether sleep is evading you or not, if you stop and spend time dwelling on what He has given you rather than what He hasn't given you, you will be blessed and He will give you peace.

Psalm 21 | Psalm 94 | Proverbs 12:25 | Ephesians 1

Six - Shopping Days

So how many shopping days are left? Sorry to stress you out. Or maybe now is the time to get stressed out! *Who will you buy for? From where will the money come? When will you get the decorations on the house? Where will you have Christmas dinner? Will you have anyone with whom to share it? Will you be invited to anyone's home? Will you be alone on Christmas day?* Those questions are wild aren't they? It should not be this way, but it is. Christmas is a hectic season that seems to get longer and more intense each year.

Can we offer a few thoughts and maybe some suggestions? They may have been said before, but they may be new to you. We thought this would be the time to say, *"Peace to all those who stress out over Christmas!"* and give you a few pointers:

- Memorize three words and say them to yourself when you get in your car, and turn the ignition switch each day between now and Dec. 24th. Here they are, *"Jesus started this."* By "this," we do not mean the Christmas holiday. We mean *all* of this. Through Him, all things were created. He came to save us from our sin. As you start the car, try to remember, *"Jesus started this."* That may move you towards thinking, praising and other good things.
- Think about this as you pull out your credit or debit card to buy a gift. In fact, you could write it and tape it to your card. *"Jesus*

purchased redemption." He bought the souls of mankind on the cross of Calvary. Corny? Maybe it is. But is it helpful to your soul as a reminder? Try it.

- If you are old fashioned and write checks or pay with cash, perhaps you could be reminded as you pay for purchases that, *"Jesus paid it all."* He paid for every sin of those He loves. It is the "why" of Christmas.

- As you think about with whom you will spend Christmas, perhaps you would remember the number "3." The fellowship of the Trinity: *the Father giving the Son, the Son sacrificing for His friends and the Spirit moving to change hearts.*

I am sure you can think of many other ways that you can shift the focus to Jesus. From past personal failure, we can tell you that it is hard to do. A plan can be helpful, if you lay it out early. Then you can then enjoy the season, being grounded in your faith, washing your mind with the water of the word as you traverse over the valley and through the woods to grandmother's house.

Psalm 29 | John 14:26-28 | Jude 1:2

_____

_____

_____

_____

_____

_____

_____

Seven - The Coming of a King

I remember being around 7 years old when my uncle took me out for the day. It was in the very early days of the 1960's. I do not recall him saying where we were going. But we ended up at a place swarming with excited people. The crowd lined the road on both sides. I do not remember the specific details, but I recall the crowd all looking in one direction and someone saying, "Here he comes!" It was the President of the United States.

I think I caught a glimpse of him as his motorcade sped by, but what I most remember was the crowd. How they cheered and how they waved. The excitement was electric and tangible. I felt it, and I knew that the man in that car was honored, loved and respected. After he passed by, the crowd dispersed, satisfied that they had caught just a glimpse of him.

Daniel saw the Lord coming towards the Ancient of Days, and all power, glory, honor and rule was given to Him. Moses caught a glimpse too, as did Abraham and others. When we worship together He is in our midst. Not being able to physically see Him does not matter. The King has come, is coming and will come again. I pray that as you worship corporately during this Christmas season you would sense the Lord is with you and that He is worthy of honor, love, respect and more. And when you leave that you would say you had caught just a glimpse, and were satisfied.

Psalm 145:12-14 | Daniel 7:9-14 | Isaiah 37:15-17

Eight - Candles

I don't know anyone who hates candles. They are warm and inviting. Sometimes they smell good too. They are passive, but with a hint of danger. People like candles and many have them in their house this time of year. Some people even put fake candles in their windows! Candles are everywhere.

A few people have five of them on their dinner table. The Advent wreath is an ancient tradition. You may have seen one before; it is a round flat wreath with three purple candles, one pink candle and a white candle in the middle.

The interesting thing about these candles is that they are not all lit at the same time. One candle is lit for the first Sunday of Advent, and the next week, two candles are lit. By week four, all the candles are burning brightly. The fifth candle is lit on Christmas Eve.

So what is the story? Well, there are several stories, as it turns out, because the tradition goes back a long way. Most common is that the candles are lit to prepare us and to call us to wait. Prepare for what? Prepare our hearts for Jesus. Wait for what? Wait for Him to return. The Bible is full of candles and waiting. As Christians, we are called to look to the past with great joy and the future with great hope in spite of our circumstances. The light of the world descended into darkness and He will come again.

Now a few details: The first candle is the candle of prophecy; the prophets said he would come and we say He will come back again. The second candle is the candle of love. His love is everlasting, and we are called to love others as He has loved us. Third is the candle of joy. He suffered greatly for the joy set before Him, so that our joy may be made complete. The fourth is peace. He made peace for us with God, and we should be peacemakers.

Of course, the center candle, the Christ candle, represents the light of the world coming to chase away all darkness. He is the center of all things.

So you might want to experiment having an advent wreath. There is no magic to it. It is just a tool designed to help us focus on the One who came to save His people from their sin.

Malachi 3:1-5 | Luke 1

_____

_____

_____

_____

_____

_____

_____

_____

_____

_____

_____

_____

Nine - O Antiphons

As G.K.Chesterton once said, *"Tradition is the democracy of the dead. It is gives votes to the most obscure of all classes; those who have gone before us."*

The Benedictines went before us, and we want to take a moment to count their votes to see if we might have a majority on this topic. They introduced the O Antiphons to the church as a series of sayings to be used during the Advent season. We thought you might enjoy using them during family devotions this month.

Our ancestors have overwhelmingly said Christmas is a time to hold fast to the deep mystery of what happened and look forward to the mystery of what is to come.

The monks arranged these antiphons with a definite purpose. If one starts with the last title and takes the first letter of each one - Emmanuel, Rex, Oriens, Clavis, Radix, Adonai, Sapientia - the Latin words Ero Cras are formed. It means, *"Tomorrow, I will come."* Therefore, the Lord Jesus, whose coming we have prepared for in Advent, and whom we have addressed in these seven Messianic titles, "speaks" to us saying, *"Tomorrow, I will come."* This is, indeed, our hope. All of the prophecies are from Isaiah. We encourage you to go back and read the originals; maybe take one each day this week to meditate on.

O Sapientia (Wisdom):
"The spirit of the Lord shall rest upon him: a spirit of wisdom and of understanding, a spirit of counsel and of strength, a spirit of knowledge and fear of the Lord, and his delight shall be the fear of the Lord." (Isaiah 11:2-3)

O Adonai (Lord):
"The Lord is Our King; it is He who will save us." (Isaiah 33:22)

O Radix Jesse (Root):
"But a shoot shall sprout from the stump of Jesse, and from his roots a bud shall blossom." (Isaiah 11:1)

O Clavis David (Key):
"I will place the Key of the House of David on His shoulder; when he opens, no one will shut, when he shuts, no one will open." (Isaiah 22:22)

O Oriens (Light):
"The people who walked in darkness have seen a great light; upon those who dwelt in the land of gloom a light has shown." (Isaiah 9:2)

O Rex Gentium (King of nations):
"For a child is born to us, a son is given us; and the government shall be upon His shoulders and he will be called Wonderful Counselor, Mighty God." (Isaiah 9:6)

O Emmanuel (God with us):
"The Lord himself will give you this sign: the Virgin shall be with child, and bear a son, and shall name him Emmanuel." (Isaiah 7:14)

_____

_____

_____

_____

Ten - Christmas Music

Truth be told, some of you are not fans of Christmas music played on the radio. I know it is hard to tell your friends and family, so we can keep it as our secret. That song about the shoes really grates on your nerves doesn't it? Those Chipmunks could drive anyone up a wall. Where is your pellet gun when you need it? Bruce Springsteen should stick to rock and roll. And baby, it is *not that* cold outside!

Now for others of you, who read the last paragraph in shock, not believing anyone could be a Christmas music hater, there is nothing like Nat King Cole, Tran Siberian Orchestra or Burl Ives. Further, that little boy loved his mother and wanted to get her those shoes as a sign of his affection! As far as you are concerned, holly, jolly Christmas music should start in October and run through January, right?

I am not going to take sides, but I do want to ask us all to consider going deep. Jingle Bells may be upbeat and White Christmas nostalgic, but the words written by the great Christian hymn writers touch something deeper in our souls as we reflect on the event *and* the events to come.

So as we enter in to the season of carols, can we encourage you to think about the context in which the great hymns were written? Many of our carols were written by men and women who were passionate about the work of Christ in the world. Frank Houghton, who wrote *Thou Who Wast Rich Beyond All Splendor*, wrote it in response to the persecution of Christians in China. Isaac Watts knew as he wrote *Joy to the World* that God "ruled the world with truth and grace and made the nations prove the glories of His righteousness" because of his personal experience.

Imagine the priest who wrote *Silent Night*, starring up at the sky and seeing the beauty of God in creation; the unknown author of *O Come O Come Emmanuel* longing for the second coming, or Charles Wesley remembering his own conversion as he penned, *"God and sinners reconciled!"*

Now maybe you might take a moment and sing, yes sing these Christmas hymns; as the words soak into your soul. Then you can look for more.

O Come O Come Emmanuel (author unknown)
"O come, Thou Rod of Jesse, free
Thine own from Satan's tyranny
From depths of Hell Thy people save
and give them victory o'er the grave
Rejoice! Rejoice! Emmanuel shall come to thee, O Israel."

Angels From The Realms of Glory (James Montgomery)
"Saints before the altar bending,
watching long in hope and fear,
Suddenly the Lord, descending,
In His temple shall appear:
Come and worship, Come and worship,
worship Christ, the newborn King!"

Matthew 1:22-24 | Luke 2:12-14

_____

_____

Eleven - Advent

It is a wonderful quote:

> "St John sums up the whole life and work of Jesus this way: 'The Word became flesh and dwelt among us; and we beheld his glory, glory as of the only begotten of the Father, full of grace and truth.' That, please note, is a careful re-definition of glory. When you look at the Word becoming flesh, you do not see the sort of glory that Augustus Caesar and emperors work for. You see the glory that is the family likeness of God himself. Caesar's glory is full of brute force and deep ambiguity. God's glory – Jesus glory is full of grace and truth. The royal babe in the cowshed overturns all that the human empire stands for." N.T. Wright

Man made glory can be very shiny; but if it is not taken captive to the glory of God and if it does not point to Him, it is but tin, sure to rust. Often the glory of man has been gained by brute force and has much ambiguity as to its origins. Not so with the glory revealed in Christ Jesus. It is revealed in grace and truth.

The truth can be hard at times, can't it? You know that, if you have had to share hard news with someone. The truth is that He did become flesh and dwell among us. During this season most people do not know or believe that. So part of your holiday activity perhaps needs to be to pray for those who have not had their hearts turned to God. During this time of year many people are open.

Next you are perhaps being called to serve with love. No need to get your evangelism button out of the drawer and wear it on your sleeve. Let's assume they know that you are a Christian. If so, how would they expect you to act? Will you act with grace? Will you show love to the unlovable? Will you give to those in need? Yes, we are called to be gracious and giving and loving all the time, but this season is an opportunity to go above the normal and bless those who are not in the family of God.

You have beheld His glory, even as the disciples did by the fact that you have received Him. So now is the season for that glory should be evident. Winsomely share a good word, invite someone to dinner or even encourage them to come along to church for some special Christmas program.

While you are at it, don't forget that those who are in the family need encouragement, too? Maybe it is a Christian who is less fortunate in some way; maybe it is someone older, or a new believer, who needs to be blessed. There are plenty of opportunities. One last thing: don't stress here. Just a little bit of grace and truth will do, as you think about the babe who overturned all things to rescue you.

Psalm 24:9-10 | Isaiah 60:1-3 | Matthew 25:30-32

_____
_____
_____

Twelve - Shake Off the Dust

Do any of the worthless idols of the nations bring rain? Do the skies themselves send down showers? No, it is you, O LORD our God. Therefore our hope is in you, for you are the one who does all this. -Jeremiah 14:22

So how is the house coming along? Whether you live in an apartment or a five-bedroom house, at this time of year there is probably a bit of scenery change going on. That may mean you need to go in the basement or attic and get those decorations out. Of course you may have to re-arrange furniture a bit in order to get everything in its place. That is where the problem is first seen. Dust!

I know there are certain places in my house that I can go, behind the couch in the den for example, and see the dust that has accumulated. They are places that are off the beaten track. Places where I do not go often. Places where not much activity has happened. Places hidden from public view.

I ran across a comment by John Calvin in which he speaks of us having faith, but not perfect faith. To paraphrase, he says that we still have the "dust of unbelief" on our souls. When we sit idle and do not pursue the things of Christ, dust accumulates. That is a great word picture for me. Sanctification is, then, the process by which we "shake off the dust" of unbelief; not by ourselves, but by asking the Holy Spirit to blow gently.

To worship God I must be willing to seek the dusty places and to shake them out. I can't just simply recognize them and hope for the best. I need to look for places where the dust of greed, anxiety, fear, and other idols sits and collects. It is a bit of a messy task to clean off that dust, and I know that I cannot do it in and of myself. I need Him to show me and teach me. I need Him to motivate me to look and see. And at the end of the day, He is the one who will make the change needed.

So can I ask you if you are willing to look behind the couch? I think that you might find it refreshing at the end of the day. And the Christmas decorations will look better once you get cleaned up a bit.

John 17:16-20 | 1 Thessalonians 5:22-24 | Hebrews 9:12-14

Thirteen - Golden Gift Box

I love Christmas and all that comes with it. I love Santa, Frosty and Rudolph; giving gifts and holiday parties; all the secular parts of Christmas that really have nothing to do with the true meaning of Christmas. They can be really enjoyable and I believe are in and of themselves not a bad thing. But if we let them become a distraction from the real thing then we are missing the point.

Growing up we had a 'golden gift box'. It was the first gift put under the tree and it was the first present that my sister and I opened every year on Christmas Eve. Inside my mom had created a set of visual cues to remind us of our Savior and why we celebrate His birth. There was a small golden teapot to represent our blessings that are poured out. Golden joy bells, a set of baby toy keys spray painted gold to represent the keys to the kingdom, and a tiny Lamb's book of life where our names are written. Also included was a light bulb to represent Jesus as the light of the world, a cross for our salvation, a dove of peace and broken chains to represent our broken chain of sins, which Jesus did on the cross. He had to come to earth, take on flesh, live and die, all for us.

We went through the box every year and I am sure that there were years where we thought, "Yeah mom, okay, now how about the real presents?" But we always went through it slowly, talking through the items and what each meant to us. We talked about how Jesus was the "ultimate gift" and that the presents we give each other are supposed to serve as a reminder of our ultimate gift in Christ.

As I have grown older, I am so thankful for traditions like that. Now as an adult, I have a golden gift box at my house, too, (although mine is actually silver because that matches my Christmas decorations better) and every time I see that box I am reminded that the greatest gift I receive at Christmas is Jesus and His gift of salvation. Do you have any Christmas traditions that point you to our Savior King who came to earth to save us? If not, maybe this is the year to start one. Maybe you'll create a golden gift box or an advent wreath or who knows, you may be more creative than any of us. By all means, enjoy the Christmas season and all that it entails but don't forget to find time to focus on the true significance of Christmas.

Matthew 2 | Romans 5:14-17 | Romans 6:23

_____

_____

_____

_____

_____

_____

_____

_____

_____

_____

_____

_____

_____

_____

Fourteen - Hectic Holidays

I was walking through my local library recently and stopped at the holiday section. It was amazing to see the range of topics covered. As I looked through the various books all of them gave me the same impression. We are striving for perfection, to make everything okay. This year will be the perfect Christmas: we'll take beautiful Christmas photos, everyone will get along and the whole holiday season will be like a Norman Rockwell painting from start to finish. The truth is that nothing is ever perfect and the more that we push to make everything look perfect the less peace and enjoyment we will actually have.

Remember the first Christmas? I'm betting that was not the way that Mary and Joseph had planned for the birth of their child to go. Instead of a nice, clean and warm home, they were in a strange place, sleeping in barn. She had to put her baby in a feeding trough. Not my idea of how I'd want it to go, and yet in Luke 2:19 it says "But Mary treasured up all these things and pondered them in her heart." If she can treasure those crazy things then we can probably handle a Christmas card where not everyone's looking at the camera or burned turkey or whatever goes wrong with your holiday.

This isn't to say that we can't try to make our houses look nice or desire and try to take a nice family photo but if we allow those things to steal our joy or if we try to make them the sole focus of the holidays we'll miss it.

Since we can't do everything, maybe it would help to make a priority list of the things that are really important to you. You may find that some of the things that you're stressed the most about don't really matter to you and you can just not do them this year. Maybe this is the year you focus on a few really special things and enjoy them to the fullest. The rest either happen or not but you won't spend the season stressing about it.

Make peace your number one priority this season. Not manufactured peace, not New Age inner peace that you control, but real, true peace that comes from Jesus Christ our Savior. His peace passes all human understanding. If you let it guide your heart and mind this season you may find that it rubs off on those around you too.

Numbers 6:24-27 | Luke 2 | John 14:26-28

Fifteen - My Grandmother

My grandfather had passed away when I was young and she was left behind. So she lived alone. We visited her often. She would bake the best chocolate chip cookies in the world. We would play in the park across the street from her house. On holidays all the aunts and uncles and cousins would come too. Some summers I would spend a week or more there with her while my parents were away. She would make the best cookies. Did I say that already? We would eat a simple lunch together and talk about "those men going to the moon" or "the depression" or coal furnaces or the orphanage down the street. Eat and talk. I wish I had listened better; especially about the Depression.

Sometimes in the afternoon when I would come in from the park she would be sitting in her chair. She would have dozed off. As I slammed the screen porch door she would wake up with a start. It was then that I got it. She was alone. She was an old woman living alone. If it weren't for us coming by; for family, she would just doze off. No one would wake her. No one would talk to her.

I am sure you have had a widow in your family. Maybe you are one. Naps and chocolate chip cookies are not the full story. Feeling sorry and stopping by for pity's sake is not the story either. What is? Valuing. Loving. Listening. Learning. Much can be gleaned from those who are older in years. Maybe it is just sitting and having a simple lunch and talking. Laughing. Crying.

Since my grandmother passed away I have had a habit, whenever I enter a room and see an older person, to go and speak with them. They have much to share. More so, we have much to give back. They were here before us, they made a way, they have suffered on the road and they have made much of what we have possible. They are to be honored.

So, what about you? If you have a widow in your family, enjoy. If you don't have a widow, can we encourage you, for your benefit, to get to know one? Some widows have few relatives in town and they would love to get to know you and share stories with you. They are a blessing and you can be too. You can talk and eat at the same time.

My mother became a widow, my mother-in-law is a widow and perhaps my wife will be a widow. I know that many who are younger would benefit from spending time with her after I am gone. She now makes the best chocolate chip cookies in the world.

So, can I encourage you today to look around? Family, friends, and even in the mirror and ask what God would have you do?

Isaiah 1:16-18 | Acts 6:1-3 | 1 Timothy 5:3-5

_____

_____

_____

_____

_____

Sixteen - Tradition!

Every year for as long as I can remember we have decorated our Christmas tree listening to Bing Crosby and then Motown Christmas. We have always had plenty of different Christmas music but we never even thought about playing anything else, while putting up the tree. To this day any time that I hear "That Christmas Feeling" by Bing Crosby I am taken back to my parent's living room, Christmas lights, and ornaments with a warm nostalgic glow. I love that, I love those memories and I love that I have those traditions.

Growing up, we had lots of traditions. We used to joke that if we did it once and liked it, then it was a tradition. If we didn't, well then it was just something we did that one time. Another of my favorite traditions is the annual Christmas party with my mom's sisters and their husbands and kids. Every year at the beginning of the season we would go to my Aunt's house and we'd play or decorate Christmas cookies or whatever we decided was fun until it was time for dinner. Then we'd eat and go down to the family room to open presents. The fun thing was that we would open our Christmas PJs or matching shirt from our grandmother. Our Mawmaw always made sure she found or made some kind of matching Christmas attire for all 7 of us. Then we'd all put on the matching Christmas garb and the kids would pile on my aunt's big blue couch for a picture. Early on we barely took up half of the couch. These days we don't get matching Christmas clothes but we still take a picture on the same couch, with a few sitting on the arms or in front of the couch as we are all now adults. This year we will take that picture on the newly reupholstered couch; my aunt couldn't bear to get rid of it, because it's part of the tradition.

I love traditions, they seem to root us to others, bring back good memories. Most traditions have some level of enjoyment or else we would never keep doing them. We teach these traditions to those who are younger, our children, nieces, nephews and so on, in hopes that they will carry them on for years to come. But maybe you don't have good memories from childhood or your life is such that you can't really participate in your previous traditions. It's never too late to start traditions. Decide now that you will let the past be the past and this year you will start a new tradition; one of hope for the future.

Let us never forget that the best tradition we can have is a tradition of true faith in Christ within our families. He is the one, who has given us the gift of family, whether it is the family you were born with or one you have formed over time. That gift of family is a small taste here on earth of our heavenly family.

Romans 5: 1-5 | I Corinthians 13: 4-13 | Ephesians 2

_____

_____

_____

_____

Seventeen - Love

Sometimes it is just good to be reminded. Jesus loves you. He really does. If you have received Him as the one who saves, the one who has paid your debt, the one who is king and the one who is coming again, He loves you. In fact He loved you before you loved Him. This piece could end there. That is all that needs to be said.

But, I want to say a few more things because for most of us it is hard to know, experience, and feel the love of Jesus. In part, it is hard to feel the love of Jesus because we are broken and we live in a broken world. The reception simply is not always so good. But, there are some things that we can do to help us understand better that He loves us.

We can be honest when we aren't feeling His love. Hiding your discontent with an apparent lack of God's affection does not help, so we suggest you share it. Not in a "poison spreading" sort of way, but in a way that expresses your disappointment. Saying it, may release the pressure that is building. You don't need to play the victim, but it would be better if you did not pretend that everything is all right. You will need to find someone safe to do that with.

We can surround ourselves with things that have been known to help; great music, reading helpful books and being with godly encouraging people. Those three things have helped others know that Jesus loves them and there is no reason to think they won't help us. It is important to choose carefully so you might get some suggestions from people you spiritually respect.

We can go to the Bible and combine it with prayer. Note I said combine. When you don't feel loved, reading the Bible can be a bit flat. So, pray and say "I want to hear from You God and know You are real". If you get in the Word and ask God to meet you, He will open your eyes to the truth. Don't just open the Bible and pick a passage and hope for divine inspiration, but we do recommend you take time to immerse yourself in the Word and see what the Story of Jesus is really all about, from Genesis to Revelation.

Lastly, we could ask ourselves the hard question, "Do I love Him?" Sometimes, if a relationship has gone cold, it is my fault. What do you do if that is the case? You do the same things. Be honest, surround yourself and go to the Word. You might also throw a little repentance in there somewhere. Along the way, the flame will be lit because the reality is He does love you.

That is where we started, isn't it?

Psalm 119:158-160 | John 15:8-18 | 1 John 4:18-20

_____
_____
_____
_____
_____
_____

Eighteen - Are You Singing Off Key?

Our church staff gets together once a week to pray for requests that come during the week. We get together on Tuesdays and spend about 45 minutes praying for these requests (among other things). In preparation to pray, we often sing a bit and listen to the Word.

Just before Christmas, I happened to be standing next to someone in staff prayer. Let's call her "Jackie" just to protect her identity. Anyway, as we were singing, I felt like my voice and hers were not in synch. It sounded odd and scratchy. I thought, "Is she singing off-key a bit?" I kept on going, as did she. I kept hearing this slightly off-key voice though. I thought it must be her, but I knew she was a good singer. But, it seemed to be her. I was conflicted. I had seen her up front leading the congregation in worship. So, I thought she must have a decent voice, but yet it sounded so "off".

There was only one way to make sure, so I did it. I stopped singing. Oddly, the poorly pitched voice went away. It was me. I was out of synch with her. Now I had a decision to make. Do I just not sing? Or, do I continue singing, knowing that I was the one with the problem? I sang. I tried to get my voice a little more in synch with hers. And you know what? She never said anything to me. She may not even remember the event. My guess is that she often has poorly pitched people standing next to her.

Here is the reality for me; I am the one off-key. If I will silence myself, I can listen to Him and hear that He is speaking beautiful and clear truth. Not one note is off-key, just perfect pitch. So if you are hearing something that seems to be dissonant, check your heart first. Then, can I encourage you to listen to His voice? Maybe even try to get in synch with what you are hearing Him say. Don't worry about perfect pitch because the good news is that He won't belittle you, or laugh at your attempt. Why? Because, "The LORD your God is with you, he is mighty to save. He will take great delight in you, he will quiet you with his love, he will rejoice over you with singing" (Zephaniah 3:17).

Ezekiel 11:18-20 | Luke 6:44-46 | 2 Thessalonians 2:16-17

Nineteen – Home

Dorothy in the Wizard of Oz said it: "There is no place like home!" Better still, Perry Como, The Carpenters and others sing of it this time of year, "...for the holidays you can't beat home, sweet home!"

Home means different things to different people. For some, the sweet aroma of cookies baking and the crackling of a fire bring back memories of beautiful evenings with friends and family. For others, home conjures up less appealing images: a family argument, too much to drink for Uncle Ned and overcooked ham. In either case, we all know that deep down inside we want and need home. We want to feel safe and be loved. We want to be cared for and have someone around who will listen to us. We want to be nurtured and we want to feel that we are part of a family.

At this time of year many people do an amazing job of decorating their homes. You may visit some of them. The decorations are meant to mark the season and to enhance the warmth of the home. Perhaps you decorate your house and then go look at others.

Now I wonder, as you walk around other people's homes, if you are bit jealous? After all, "That tree is gorgeous. Those angel figurines are divine and the table setting is to die for!" Hmm. Did we just kill the spirit of this whole thing? On the contrary, we say, let your desires outstrip your pocketbook. What? Yes, as you visit homes this season and see the beautiful decorations, I want to ask you to look at the beauty and feel the fact that it is costly.

It is fine to long for something that you cannot purchase. Why? Because, that thought may take you to the heart of the season: Something was purchased that you could not afford; something grander than angel figurines and the finest china. Jesus came to purchase you. You are the decoration. You are the gift. All that is needed is a home to put you in.

He has even taken care of that. He has prepared an eternal home for those who look to Him; a place where it is safe and all will feel love and care. That home is what you are longing for; to be close to Him; to feel His love and to celebrate being in His family.

So if you have roamed this year, now may be the time to enter back in. C.S. Lewis once said, "If I find in myself desires that the world cannot meet, it must mean I was made for another world." That is exactly what we believe. We were made for another world and mysteriously, that world has in part collided with our world by a baby being born in, not a home, but a stable.

Matthew 7:10-12 | 1 Corinthians 6:19-20 | 2 Corinthians 9:14-15

_____
_____
_____

Twenty - Release us!

This hymn is sung in most churches over the holiday season.

> *"Come thou long expected Jesus, born to set thy people free. From our fears and sins release us; let us find our rest in Thee."* – Come Thou Long Expected Jesus, Charles Wesley

There is so much to unpack in just two short lines. Are we really longing for Jesus to come again or if He showed up would we say "Oh Jesus thanks for coming but I am super busy this week and actually next week, too. Maybe you could come back in a month or so?" Okay, that's a ridiculous exaggeration and hopefully none of us would say that to Jesus' face, but are we essentially doing that through our lives each day? We busily run from task to task and some days never even think of Him. The good news: God loves us anyway. Even more good news: it is never too late to find our rest in Christ. He holds the power to release us from sin and to wipe away every fear. All we have to do is rest in Him.

If that sounds easier said than done, that's because it isn't easy and it isn't a onetime thing. As humans we are prone to wander and forget that our hope and rest is in Christ. That's why regular time in the Word and in communion with God is so important.

We often become so consumed and focused on the world around us that we miss the bigger picture.

This can especially be true at the holidays. In Luke 2:25, the scriptures talk about a man named Simeon, "It had been revealed to him by the Holy Spirit that he would not die before he had seen the Lord's Messiah". So he waited, anxiously anticipating His arrival and when the spirit moved him, he went to the temple and saw the Lord and his response was profound: "Sovereign Lord, as you have promised, you may now dismiss your servant in peace" (Luke 2:29). He didn't ask for more time or anything else. His soul was at peace and life was complete.

Mark 13:33 reminds us "Be on guard! Be alert! You do not know when that time will come." Let's remember today that this world is fleeting. For today at least, let's fix our eyes on the world to come and live our lives preparing for the day when He returns.

Psalm 33:21-22 | Luke 2:22-40 | 2 Timothy 4:7-9

Twenty One - Sleep in Heavenly Peace?

I was given a spa gift certificate a few months ago and recently used it. One of the first things that I noticed as I walked into the spa was that the majority of the spa was in semi-darkness, dimly lit, very quiet, and everyone spoke softly. I found that it made me feel calmer and helped me to relax as I prepared for my spa service. I have taken that idea home and now try to have times where I turn off most or all of the lights and light a few candles and sit in silence or with very quiet soft music. Christmas is a great time to do this because you can use your Christmas tree for dim light.

As I sit, I like to do two things. First, think and pray through the things that are heavy on my heart and give them to the Lord. In 1 Peter 5:7 the scripture says "Cast all your anxiety on him because he cares for you". So I cast my cares to Him and then I let go of them - or at least I strive to let go. Then I like to reflect on all the things in my life that I can be thankful for. It doesn't have to be huge things, it can be simple things like being thankful to have a few minutes to sit and reflect. This is a great thing to do before going to bed or at the start of the day. Take a few minutes, shut off the TV and all the noise of the world and be still. Psalm 46:9a says "Be still, and know that I am God". I know that this is easier said than done, but just as with anything else it gets easier every time that you try.

Here's a quick list to go through to get you started:
1. Pray for things that are worrying you
2. Pray for heart change where there is sin
3. Thank the Lord for the blessings in your life
4. Pray for eyes to see all the blessings He gives you that you have missed.

Today, why not take 5 minutes to be still and quiet and see how God moves you.

1 Chronicles 16:33-35 | Psalm 7:17 |
1 Thessalonians 5:16-18

Twenty Two - Holiday Giving

We all want the holidays to be a time of joy, family, laughter, giving and receiving - as they should be! We should go to someone's house for dinner; we should celebrate, and we should cherish the time we have with loved ones. A point should be made to give gifts and to give a little something to those who have less.

For some, this may be the hardest holiday season ever. Jobs may be scarce and anxiety about money is high. You may be nervous about spending money or may, in fact, not have any to spend. Times are tight. Now, you might think that I could encourage you and say things like, "O well we have each other and our health. Those are the important things!" or "What is important is being together, not the gifts you get or give." Those would be true and good words, but I am not going to say them.

Frank Houghton, during the darkest of days on the mission field in China wrote this,

> *Thou who wast rich beyond all measure,*
> *All for love's sake becamest poor*
> *Thrones for a manger didst surrender,*
> *Sapphire-paved courts for stable floor.*
> *Thou who wast rich beyond all splendour,*
> *All for love's sake becomes poor.*
>
> *Thou who art God beyond all praising,*
> *All for love's sake becamest man;*
> *Stooping so low, but sinners raising*

Heavenwards by thine eternal plan.
Thou who art God beyond all praising,
All for love's sake becamest man.

When we remember that He became poor, then we can enter into our poverty and see that we are called by "the poor one" to give freely of whatever we do have: our time, a cup of tea, a hug, a bowl of soup, or a smile to others in His name and for His kingdom's sake. When we do that and when we are grateful for Him, in His state of poverty, we do not waste our hard economic time.

So can I encourage you to not waste the "less" that you have? Look to Him and see that He is all we need. Have a warm and wonderful holiday.

Proverbs 22:2 | Isaiah 14:30 | 2 Corinthians 9:8-10

_____

_____

_____

_____

_____

_____

_____

_____

_____

_____

_____

_____

_____

Twenty Three – What? No Lights?

One of my favorite Christmas traditions every year with my husband is to pick up Christmas coffees or hot chocolate and drive around the city looking at Christmas lights. We listen to Christmas music and discuss the ones that we like the best and why. We really like the spiral Christmas tree displays that have been showing up a lot recently and think that the giant inflatables are generally overused (although we have a friend who uses them and they look great), but that's just us. This past year we noticed that there were a bunch of houses that did not have any Christmas lights out and I said to my husband, "Where is their Christmas Spirit? Can you believe they don't have any lights?" Then we drove up to our own home and realized that we were like most of those homes. Other than candles in the windows we had no lights on the outside of our house either. So if we weren't doing it, how could we be judging others for doing the same thing? Oops.
So after Christmas I bought décor for our lawn and this Christmas we will be ready.

But all of this got me thinking, do I do this in other areas of my life? Do I hold others to an ideal standard that I am not even trying to meet?

The truth is that God's standard finds us all lacking. The standard is perfection (Matthew 5:48) and none of us are perfect, as much as we hate to admit it. But that's why He sent his Son, to save us, to pay the debt that we could never pay, to make us blameless in His sight. He loved us so much that He came to earth to save us and the cost to save us was so high that no one else could do it and we could never pay it on our own. That's the true meaning of Christmas: that Christ came to save us because we cannot save ourselves.

In the midst of the lights, decorations, gifts and parties; let's remember to give thanks to our Lord for the wonderful gift of His love and salvation.

Psalm 27:1-3 | John 3:1-21 | Romans 6:23 | Hebrews 5:7-10

_____

_____

_____

_____

_____

_____

_____

_____

_____

_____

_____

_____

_____

_____

_____

_____

_____

_____

Twenty Four - A Little Love

It's the classic scene at the end of "A Charlie Brown Christmas" where Linus says, "I never thought it was such a bad little tree. It's not bad at all really; maybe it just needs a little love". Then all the Peanuts characters scramble their arms around and magically turn the sad little tree into a beautifully decorated tree. Charlie Brown then comes out and sees what all his friends have done for him. I love this scene, but in truth I love the whole special. It's a young boy searching for the true meaning of Christmas, beyond the presents and commercialism. His friends give him many possible theories: presents, money, being happy but Charlie Brown isn't buying it. Then Linus tells him the true meaning of Christmas out of Luke 2.

I have heard that even back in the 60s when this was originally made there was some discussion over whether or not to use the Luke 2 reference. But Peanuts creator, Charles Schultz, was adamant saying "If we don't tell the true meaning of Christmas, who will?"

The same is true for all of us. If we will not share with others the true meaning of Christmas, of Christ's love for us and the gift of eternal life then who will?

This year, I want to keep always on my heart the love of the Father and give it away to those around me. Look around for ways to share God's love. Bring cookies to someone who is lonely. Help out with winter chores for the elderly neighbors, or give shoebox or angel tree gifts for the needy. There are more ways to share the love of Jesus than time, so pick some and do them. You will be as blessed as those you are serving.

All they need is a little love. How will you give it away this year?

Luke 2 | Titus 3:4-5 | 1 John 4:6-7

_____
_____
_____
_____
_____
_____
_____
_____
_____
_____
_____
_____

Twenty Five - Underneath

As we approach Christmas we thought it could be a good time to reflect on what is underneath. It is so easy for us to get caught up in all the events and activities of Christmas: trees and decorations; presents and food; trying to decide if you should switch to low fat eggnog. Not that there is anything intrinsically wrong with those things, but we want to be sure we remind you to focus on what is underneath.

It is Jesus.

He is the One who is center stage and the One to whom we must give our affection. Anything less would be unhealthy for us, and a dishonor to Him. So we want to invite you to take a short time out. It could be as little as ten minutes. We would love for you to open a bible and read the story of Christmas by yourself. It may be very familiar to you or maybe you have never read it in its entirety. It does not matter. Can we encourage you to read it again? Just get to a quiet space and take time to let it soak in. It is rich.

We believe the Word of God is living and active and that includes the Christmas narrative. We believe it can re-instill hope in your heart and help you to see reality. We think if you will take time to be with Him this week, He will bless you and remind you that He came for you. He will gently whisper that He calls you to come to the manger, come to the cross and then go to those He loves for His namesake and bless them in His name. It could be a moment to cherish. It could change the rest of the week for you.

Some of you will be alone for Christmas. Others will be with people who are hard to deal with. Many will celebrate well with friends and family. Whatever your context is, we want to encourage you to put Christ in the center. He is the one who is the light of the world and your heart. He came for you.

Soon it will all be over. The tree will come down and the lights will be turned off; but not this week. This week is a week for you to reflect on the incarnation of Jesus, the Word made flesh; the One who dwelt among us.

Luke Chapters 1 and 2

Twenty Six - The Toy You Had to Have

One year my sister wanted "the toy of the year"; she wanted a Go Go My Walking Pup. In the tradition of Cabbage Patch Kids and Tickle Me Elmo demand far out stripped the supply of the toys. My parents searched high and low for one to no avail. Then on Christmas Eve a friend called to say that she had found an extra one. One catch, she was in the next state over. So my parents dropped us off at a friend's house on Christmas Eve and drove to get the toy my sister had to have. They were so excited to be able to give her the toy she really wanted and looked forward to watching her open it the next day. On Christmas morning, she tore off the wrapping and screamed with joy and surprise that the toy she wanted was hers. Everyone was so happy and it was a great Christmas.

You know what I'm going to tell you next right? Yep, a few weeks after Christmas that toy had been relegated to the forgotten toys pile. It turns out that the commercial made it seem much easier to use and maneuver. Basically the dog went forwards and back and sometimes struggled to do that. So we played with it some but it didn't live up to everything she'd hoped it would be.

Does it seem as though our lives are like this a lot? We hope, pray, and strive for something. When we get it we are so happy. Then it isn't everything we'd hoped it would be so we are disappointed. As adults things are not typically as simple as I want a toy and God gives it to me. Prayers don't get answered like that, at least not typically. Instead, often what I think I want gets changed as the Lord changes my heart. That thing that I thought I couldn't live without now holds no interest to me or maybe it does but I have a whole new perspective on it.

It's okay to desire things but whom or what is our hope in? Is our hope in things however improbable working out in our favor or is our hope in the Giver of all good gifts? I know what I want my hope in.

Romans 8:23-25 | 1 Corinthians 15:18-20 | 1 Thessalonians 2:18-20

Twenty Seven - Silent Night

Lo in the silent night
A child to God is born.
And all is bought again
That here was lost, forlorn

Could but thy soul o man
Become a silent night?
God would then be born in thee
And set all things aright
-source unknown, modernized by R. Schlichting

The original source of this quote is somewhat obscure, but in any case I modernized it for us. I would love for you to read it aloud slowly, trying to get the rhyme when you are in a place that you feel comfortable in doing so.

It may first remind you of the hymn, Silent Night. But look again. Imagine the night He was born. A purchase began on that night to buy what had been lost. The word forlorn means, forsaken, and nearly hopeless. That is what it was like before the Son came to make all things right. People were desperate. And then He came as a child, grew to be a man and lived perfectly. He died a beautiful death that we might be set free.

Read the second stanza again if you will. Just as the night became silent to receive the once and future king, could your heart again become silent? There is a lot of noise during the holiday season and the author is calling for us to be still in the midst of it.

He may be speaking to those who have never received Him as Savior, God would then be born in the, and he may be talking to those who need a re-birth of sorts, a re-kindling of the gospel in their hearts. In either case, when He comes He sets all things right.

That is what we need this season. To have all things be set right. That does not mean that all of our troubled relationships will be restored or our circumstances will change. It means that in our souls we will rest in the fact that He is good and He loves us. We can be silent and receive what He has for us in light of that.

So, can your soul become a silent night for sixty seconds? We pray it can.

Psalm 31:23-24 | Micah 7:7 | Romans 5:1-3

_____

_____

_____

_____

_____

_____

_____

_____

_____

_____

_____

_____

_____

Twenty Eight - Broken Glass

I had a roommate once who loved to work with stained glass. Nothing big like what you would see at St. Paul's Cathedral, but he did small pieces for friends and family. One day, he showed me how it was done. Each piece of glass was carefully chosen and then cut to match the next piece. Next he wrapped a foil around the rough edge of the cut piece and heated it up with a small blowtorch as he deftly applied some solder to the mix. The two became one. He then went on to the next piece.

Initially, I could not tell what was being formed or what the picture was. But, over time it became apparent. When it was done, it was a beautiful red rose surrounded by a white background. When we held it up to the light, it became both dazzling and peaceful at the same time. It was a beautiful work completed.

Maybe you are reading today, and your life is shattered. Perhaps things have happened to you that should not have, or you have done things you regret. As you sit here, you may be thinking that your future is black and dark because your past has been. You might see yourself as a shard of glass that has no use, no future and no hope. You are just broken.

Well, you are right on one count. You are a shard of glass. We are all broken pieces of glass: jagged, rough and in need of a loving hand to pick us up, cut us to size, and wrap some foil paper around our edges. If you are thinking you have no use, future or hope, we want to encourage you to look to the One who puts together the grand mosaic we call the Kingdom.

He will make the rough places smooth as you submit to His loving care. He will wrap you up and give you a place of great importance. He may put a little heat on the situation, but it is always designed for His good purposes. He knows, as well as you may secretly know, that the picture cannot be complete without you in it. When He does complete the work, He will hold us all up to the One for whom we have been made, and it will be both dazzling and peaceful.

So you are not worthless, in whatever place or situation you find yourself today. We invite you to give yourself up to the Craftsman, God the Father, and come join the community of His people. One note of caution; we too are broken glass, sinners, in need of His hand. Sometimes we even scrape against one another and it hurts a bit. Sometimes it cuts, but we know we are all part of the mosaic, finer than anything adorning the windows of St. Paul's Cathedral. So we continue to build and love one another; knowing that one-day we will all shine like the sun before Him. As you come across stained glass this holiday season and beyond, remember your part in the mosaic and let His light shine through you.

John 1:1-18 | 1 Corinthians 1: 1-9 | 1 John 1

Twenty Nine - Will He Come?

Christmas Eve is special in our house. I am so looking forward to the night! Our whole neighborhood sets out luminaries (bags with sand and candles for the uninitiated). On the drive back from church I see candles that have been lit by other neighbors glowing along the side of the road. It warms my heart and causes it to race at the same time. When I pull into our driveway I quickly walk into the house and I smell it: Christmas Eve dinner, prime rib. Dorothy cooks it to perfection and I cannot even describe to you all the trimmings. It is amazing. And then there is desert! I hear the Christmas music playing amidst the laughter of daughters and mothers. I know my part so I enlist a daughter and light our luminaries and then a fire in the fireplace. Dinner is served!

After dinner we will walk down the street to our friend's house and he will read "The Night Before Christmas" to my kids. He has done that for 14 years in a row. It will be a great evening. Even as I write, I wish it were here. We will be together and there will be great joy.

The word Advent is from the Latin ad, which means "to" and vent, which means "come." That is pretty simple: To come. That is what we look for during this season; the coming. We do celebrate the birth of Christ and reflect on His ministry on earth as well as His death and resurrection. But more so, we should look towards the future. We want Him to come to reclaim and redeem all things finally and fully.

I wonder if that helps you or if it takes the wind out of the Christmas Season? For me it is a bit convicting. I do get wrapped up in parties, decorations, food, gifts and family reunions during this time of year so much that I forget to look forward. In fact I can be pretty content with the "now" and not think so much about what is to come.

Just as we prepare for Christmas Eve this year, we should prepare for the second coming of Christ. How do we do that? Well Paul in his letter to the Thessalonians helps us. He says, "Since we belong to the day, let us be self controlled, putting on faith and love as a breastplate and the hope of salvation as a helmet." We are called to prepare as a bride prepares for a wedding, as a mother cooks for Christmas dinner, as a father and daughters light luminaries. We are called to live as citizens of the city to come when He descends in all His glory and brings with Him the new heaven and new earth. We will all be together and there will be great joy. He will come and what a feast it will be when he does!

Psalm 38:21-22 | Psalm 62: 4-6 | Mark 1: 14-16

_____
_____
_____
_____
_____
_____

Thirty – He Has Everything

So how much do you have left to buy? Maybe a better question is, "How much do you have left to spend?" In a few days, you will be giving and receiving. We all know that the giving and receiving of gifts at Christmas time is a reflection of the great gift we have received in Christ. It is good to give gifts of time and treasure to those around. We especially want to remember those who are less fortunate.

Do you know what your loved ones want and/or need? Men are hard to buy for, especially dads. My kids ask me every year. I know I may be one of the harder people for whom to buy a gift. Socks, some underwear and maybe a new belt are my kind of gifts. This year, I really would like a DVD set of my favorite TV show and a significant gift certificate to the smoothie shop in town, but that is about it.

So what about Him? Have you thought about what you might bring Him this Christmas? After all, it is His birthday. I am not advocating gold, frankincense or myrrh. The later is very hard to find these days in any case. So what will you give Him?

I wonder if we can challenge you all this year. Give Him, Jesus, a gift. What do you get for the God who became man and has everything? Do you need ideas? Well, first of all, think about what His love language might be. Could it be time spent, acts of service or words of affirmation? It is something to think about. Perhaps Jesus' list might include these: "Love my people a bit more (act of service); listen to me by reading the Bible, talk to me from time to time (time spent), or put some of your idols down and see me more as the King (words of affirmation)." You get the idea.

Now here is the challenge: write it out and put it in an envelope with His name on it.

"Jesus, for your gift this year, in special celebration of Your birth on earth, I want to give you:

_____

_____

_____

_____

_____. I know I will fail, and I will need the Spirit to empower me; but I give this to you as a gift, as an offering!"

First thing Christmas morning, open His presents. Read the cards to one another. It is His birthday. Then, share amongst yourselves and enjoy.

Romans 11:28-36 | 2 Corinthians 9:6-15

_____

_____

_____

_____

_____

_____

_____

_____

Thirty One - Rights

You have them. The right to remain silent. The right to bear arms. The right to free speech. The right to own property. You have rights in this country. People have actually fought and died so you can have rights. That is freedom. We in America celebrate freedom. It was hard won. Independence from tyrannical rule is a wonderful thing.

Now here is the twist and it comes in two forms. The first is a question. Are you living under tyrannical rule? We don't mean in the political sense. We mean in the spiritual sense. Are you living under the direction of your sin nature that says, "Do this!" and "Do that!" Are you responding to that which is dark and that which really wants to keep you in bondage? It could be in the shape of a bottle, or a credit card or a naked woman on a screen. It may come to you in the shape of a shopping mall or a weight scale. Perhaps it is a sneaky idol like jealousy or discontent with your lot. Whatever it is, we say, "Down with tyranny!" This is a day we call you to live as free men and women because Christ has set you free.

The second form of twist is this: you do not have to use your rights. Even in the examples above, you could talk, not own a gun or not talk. By definition, a right means that you may or may not do it. You don't have to. *You can lay down your rights.* Here we enter into the fuller mystery of the gospel. Jesus had all power and all rights. He did not live under tyranny, giving in to the dark side. He was perfectly and joyfully obedient. We call that the active righteousness of Christ. Then He laid down His right to life that He might overcome the tyrannical rule of another. He accomplished it. We call that His passive righteousness.

So because the great freedom fighter came to set us free on both counts, we are able, by His power to resist the temptation to live in bondage *and* we can enjoy the full freedom that comes in laying down our rights joyfully for the sake of others. That is freedom!

**1 Corinthians 8| 1 Corinthians 9:1-15 |
1 John 3:11-24**

Thirty Two - There Is Still Time

The countdown to Christmas seems like it started in October. Now, it is nearly here. However, there is still time. You might be asking, "Time for what?" Well, you have time to go back to the store. For some of you, that thought is ridiculous. For some of you, that is certain. There may really be a few more things to pick up, even if just from the grocery store. Get some cranberries or sweet potatoes. Maybe you still have not purchased that one gift for that special someone. So, go if you must, or if you want. The stores will close on Christmas Eve. The countdown is almost done.

We would love for you to continue, or begin, another countdown as the shopping season ends. Begin a countdown to Christ. This one does not have days or hours attached to it because it is a countdown that continues. We wait with our candles lit, with our voices lifted, and with our hearts hopeful. We wait for Him to come, or us to go. We wait knowing there is still some time but not knowing how much.

In the Dickens classic, "A Christmas Carol," Ebenezer Scrooge is shown the past, present and future in a new light. While it is not a gospel narrative in many ways, Dickens points to something central to the gospel at this time of year. Seeing his sin, Scrooge begs for a chance to change, a chance to be different. The "ghostliest" of the spirits takes him to a dark place, but he does not leave him there. In a dramatic scene, Scrooge says, "Your nature intercedes for me and pities me. Assure me that I may yet change these shadows you have shown me by an altered life!" He is on his face, and the petition is granted. Did Scrooge just "will to change?" Maybe he did, but it seems the spirits somehow enabled him.

If there was a sequel, perhaps we would see him reverting to his old miserly ways. We would enter the story here. Some of you have had an encounter with the Spirit. Change has happened, yet you know that the nature of Scrooge is still with you. Petition again; He intercedes for you. Some of you are just now seeing what the Spirit is showing you. We are glad and say "Keep coming!" Some of you may be wondering, "Is there a Spirit?" For everyone, we hope that the verses today will be helpful as you think about your past, present and future. There is time, time to go to a store where we can buy gold refined in the fire. This purchase will enable us to make things right with the One we have offended, to ask forgiveness for not loving well, and to say, "I love you." There is still time, but we do not know how much.

The baby born on Christmas Eve, the second person in the Trinity, is the One who brought change. The third person, the "ghostly" Spirit, is the One who presses it into the hearts of Scrooges like us. It is good to admit we are misers: misers in our natural man and misers who are the recipients of the grandest gift. So, the countdown to Christ continues. A milepost on the way will be the candlelight services held all over the world on Christmas Eve.

Isaiah 55 | Mark 13:32-35

Thirty Three - Inexpressible Joy

I knew he was going to lose it. I was to officiate the wedding of the daughter of a close friend of mine. The night before the wedding we had the rehearsal in the chapel. What a great setting. The groomsmen and bridesmaids took their places on stage. We recessed out and then practiced coming in to the music. As my friend walked his daughter down the aisle it hit him. He began to tear up as he approached the front of the chapel. We paused. It was a wonderful moment.

Why did he cry? Well, he told me that they were not tears of sadness. He likes the guy his daughter married. He told me that they were tears of inexpressible joy. He went on to explain that sometimes words cannot express how we feel. Tears can. The thought of his daughter, the bride, marrying the man she loves, the bridegroom, brought him to tears of inexpressible joy.

Now as Christians, there is something deeper that is happening in a marriage ceremony. It is a picture. We see it in the 21st chapter of Revelation, *"I saw the Holy City, the new Jerusalem, coming down out of heaven from God, prepared as a bride beautifully dressed for her husband. And I heard a loud voice from the throne saying, 'Look! God's dwelling place is now among the people, and he will dwell with them. They will be his people, and God himself will be with them and be their God.'"*

Imagine the Father, seeing the bridegroom (His son

Jesus) as the bride (the church) comes forward at the end of time for the consummation of all things. That will be a moment of inexpressible joy and that may well be why He will wipe every tear away. It will be a joyous occasion.

For now, we are called to look for a glimpse. We may see it in a daughter's wedding. A Christmas Eve service with candles and joyful voices singing praise to God might give us a taste. We might find it as someone we know comes to faith. We may experience it as our souls are healed through confession, repentance and forgiveness. It is just a glimpse of glory and there is more to come. He is the God who gives inexpressible joy.

Romans 12: 11-13 | Colossians 1:3-12 | Jude 1:17-25

Thirty Four - Does It Matter?

For many, it has been a hard year. Many have suffered. People were born and people have died. In a way, it may feel like a repeat of the last year, the year before or ten years ago. What difference does a year make as people reflect again on the fact that 2,000 years ago Jesus came as a baby to a young mother and father? What difference does it make that He grew up as a man, lived a perfect life and died a brutal death to save His people from their sins? What does it matter that He rose from the grave and ascended into heaven? Maybe it does not matter. Perhaps it does not make a difference that He lived, died and rose again.

Now as that paragraph shocks your system, can we say something? It really may not matter. You see, all Jesus is and all He did does not matter if you have not received the gift of Him. If you have not said something like, "He is the choicest one!" or "I am in need of only what He has to give me!" then it doesn't matter. He is yesterday's news, and the last year, the last ten years or the next twenty years do not matter. Outside of Christ nothing matters. Outside of Christ, there is just "Christmas, another year over," as John Lennon wrote. Unless you have repented and turned to Him, it does not matter.

We want it to matter for you. We want you to look back on this year and know that it made a difference because He is the "fact of the matter," and we are one year closer to Him returning in glory. He is why this year mattered. He is the hope to whom we cling.

He is why we can cry out, even as we look back on an "annus horribilus," and say, "Thank you Lord Jesus" and "Come Lord Jesus! Make all things right!"

So as you turn the page on this year, can we ask you to check your heart and see if it matters? We believe He is calling His own to come with him to the next year of the King.

We long for your life, the "anno domine" we just completed, and the year to come to matter. It was, is and will be a year of the King. Long live the King!

Matthew 28:1-5 | 1 Corinthians 15

_____
_____
_____
_____
_____
_____
_____
_____
_____
_____
_____
_____
_____
_____
_____

Thirty Five - No Resolution

Well, do you dare? Do you dare to not make a New Year's resolution? It seems that everyone has at least one: Exercise more! Read more! Or find a new job! There must be something you want to resolve to do in the New Year, and January is a good time for a fresh start, right?

Actually, it probably is not the best time to start. Statistics show that most resolutions are not kept for more than a few weeks. That is the cold truth, so you might not want to bother. That is not "reverse psychology." It is just a fact. Now, instead of making a resolution, perhaps we could think about why we cannot keep resolutions.

How about this as a resolution: "Resolve: To find out why I do not keep resolutions!" Are you interested? God says we should not make a vow, and then break it. He does seem to be interested in us keeping our word. Maybe that is a good place to start.

The Lord does not change; He decrees, and it happens. He wills, and it comes to pass. He has created us in His image and for His pleasure, and He has prepared acts of service that we might walk in them. He has also created us to be dependent on Him. So what are we saying? Jesus is the one who is the covenant keeper. Christ in you is both the hope of glory and the One that you are to live through by faith. Belief is what you need, and He is the one to give it.

Let us try this: "Resolve: To believe!" What do we need to believe? No, who do we need to believe? We need to believe Him. If you "work" to that end this year, you may see other things come together. Ask Him for faith to believe that the word of God is living and active. When you get it, you may find yourself hungry for study of the Word. Ask Him for faith that He will supply all your needs according to His riches, and as it grows you may find yourself less anxious about the future. When you find yourself not believing, repent. Make that your resolution: to believe and repent, and then use the means of grace, the Word, prayer and the sacraments, to help.

Does it sound strange? Maybe it is a bit unorthodox. We might refer back to the Gospel of John. When they asked Jesus in John 6 what they needed in order to do the work God required, He said, "Believe in the one He sent." It can't hurt, can it? Resolve: to believe!

Matthew 8:5-13 | Mark 9:22-24 | Acts 10:42-44

_____
_____
_____
_____
_____
_____
_____
_____
_____
_____
_____
_____

Made in the USA
Lexington, KY
11 November 2012